Destiny's HAND

Volume 1

PIRATES
ON THE HIGH SEAS!

Destiny's HAND

VOLUME 01

Written by Nunzio DeFilippis and Christina Weir
Illustrated by Melvin Calingo

Destiny's HAND

VOLUME 1

story by **Nunzio DeFilippis and Christina Weir**   art by **Melvin Calingo**

STAFF CREDITS

toning	**Pat Aguasin**
lettering / graphic design	**Jon Zamar**
	Gabe Dela Cruz
cover design	**Nate Legaspi**
assistant editor	**Adam Arnold**
editor	**Jason DeAngelis**
publisher	**Seven Seas Entertainment**

Visit us online at www.gomanga.com.

ISBN 1-933164-35-2

Printed in Canada

First printing: December, 2006

10 9 8 7 6 5 4 3 2 1

Table of Contents

Volume 1

SPECIAL FEATURES

CHAPTER 1
Runaway Child

Three years ago...

IT'S ALL FOR SHOW. WE **NEVER** FIGHT ANYMORE.

I FOLLOW CAPTAIN BLAINE'S ORDERS.

SIGH...

AS WELL YE SHOULD, MI COMPADRE. AS WELL YE SHOULD.

CHAPTER 2
Call Of The Sea

POUNCE

HUH?

WAAH!

THEIR SHIP MAY BE UNSINKABLE, BUT WE CAN KILL THE CREW, JUST LIKE ANY...

YES SIR.

BADRU... DID YOU... DID YOU GET THE *MIRROR* FROM THE CAPTAIN'S CABIN ON THE *SAND DOLLAR?*

OF COURSE. WHAT DO YOU NEED?

GOOD, YOU'RE HERE.

I'LL REST...LATER. IT'S A PIECE... OF THE MAP... TO THE *DEVIL'S EYE.*

GOOD. THAT'S...

COUGH! COUGH!

THAT'S WHAT... MULGREW WAS AFTER. NOT... THE CARGO.

WHAT IS THERE, CAPTAIN?

ON THE BACK OF THE MIRROR... THE *FIRST* PIECE OF THE MAP... TO... *COUGH! COUGH!*

CAPTAIN, MAYBE YOU SHOULD REST.

CHAPTER 4
Heir To The Sea

WELCOME TO
ST. VICKENSBURG

DOWNTOWN   DOCKS

MILADY.

ULP.

I SEE HIM.

TUCK

THEY SEEMED FOOLED, YOUNG MISS.

YOU STILL REMEMBER YOUR WAYS AS A LADY.

I WAS NEVER A LADY, BIG GUY. NEVER.

NOW LET'S GO BREAK INTO THE GOVERNOR'S HOUSE.

CHAPTER 5
Reunion

"THE CAPTAIN HELPED HER FLEE THE CITY. AND SHE TOOK TO LIFE ON THE SEA INSTANTLY."

YOU CAN SKIRT THE EDGES OF THE STORM, USE THE WINDS TO GET SOME DISTANCE FROM ST. VICKENSBURG.

I CAN KEEP THIS SHIP FROM SINKING.

"SHE HADN'T BEEN SNEAKING OFF TO LEARN HOW TO FIGHT LIKE YOU DID, MISS SOLDANA."

"YOUNG LADY KATHERINE HAD INSTEAD INDULGED IN A VERY DIFFERENT PASTIME."

"A PASTIME I HAD SOME DIFFICULTY BELIEVING IN. MAGIC."

CAPTAIN BLAINE, I'M AFRAID THIS GIRL MAY BE CRACKED.

REALLY? I FIND HER... FASCINATING.

NO. KATHERINE, WHAT FOOLISHNESS IS THIS?

"THEN ONE DAY SHE CAME TO HIM WITH *NEWS* THAT WOULD *BREAK* HIS *HEART*."

I MUST LEAVE. I HAVE TO GO BACK AND MARRY THE GOVERNOR'S SON.

I'M *PREGNANT*, SEBASTIAN.

THAT'S WONDERFUL NEWS, BUT...

YOU DON'T UNDERSTAND. I HAVE *SEEN* OUR *FUTURE*.

THE SAME WAY I SAW YOUR ARRIVAL IN ST. VICKENSBURG THAT DAY.

EXACTLY.

YOU ARE A GOOD AND DECENT PIRATE, SEBASTIAN. A GENTLEMAN. BUT YOUR KIND IS A DYING BREED.

AND ONE DAY, YOU AND YOUR CREW WILL BE THE *LAST*.

THERE IS A TREASURE THE DEVIL'S EY

YES, I'VE HEARD OF IT. IT'S POWER IS SAID TO BE MOST *DANGEROUS*.

"WHEN SHE WAS ATTACHED, HE RECHRISTENED THE SHIP *DESTINY'S HAND*."

"CAPTAIN BLAINE HAD COMMISSIONED THE FIGUREHEAD *BEFORE* KATHERINE HAD GIVEN HIM THE BAD NEWS."

"KATHERINE DID HER BEST TO CONVINCE HIM OTHERWISE."

"HE TOLD ME ONCE LATER, AFTER SEVERAL PINTS OF MEAD, THAT THE NAME WAS MEANT TO REMIND HIM OF HIS *CURSE*."

"SHE PLACED A PIECE OF HERSELF - OF HER *SOUL*, SHE SAID - INTO LADY KATE AND ASKED HER TO *PROTECT* THE SHIP AS SHE ONCE HAD."

"HE FELT DESTINY WAS A CRUEL COMPANION, DESIGNED TO TORMENT HIM."

RUBBISH. IT'S NOT **SHIPS**. IT'S **ONE** SHIP. AND YOU KNOW WHAT I THINK OF THEIR CAPTAIN.

I **DO**. WHICH IS WHY I SUSPECT YOUR THINKING IS NOT **CLEAR** ON THIS SUBJECT.

NO ANIMALS WERE HARMED DURING THE MAKING OF THIS ACTION SEQUENCE.

About the Creators

Nunzio DeFilippis & Christina Weir

Are a writing team who have worked in comics, television, video games and film. Trained as screenwriters (DeFilippis at USCs Screenwriting Program and Weir at Emerson's Television Program), they began writing together as a team on HBO's ARLISS, where they worked for two seasons. They've also contributed two stories for Disney's KIM POSSIBLE. They joined the Seven Seas crew right from the start, creating one of the company's four launch titles, AMAZING AGENT LUNA. DESTINY'S HAND is their second book with Seven Seas. They've also worked in adapting manga from Japan, working with Del Rey on SUGAR SUGAR RUNE, GURU GURU PON CHAN and KAGETORA. In American comics, they have written SKINWALKER, THREE STRIKES, MARIA'S WEDDING, ONCE IN A BLUE MOON, THE TOMB and PAST LIES for Oni Press, and spent 3 years in the world of Marvel's mutants writing NEW MUTANTS, HELLIONS and NEW X-MEN. They have also written for WONDER WOMAN, ADVENTURES OF SUPERMAN and DETECTIVE COMICS. Their first video game project is awaiting a title and release date.

Melvin Calingo

Is the artist of Destiny's Hand. He earned a Bachelor of Fine Arts degree in the University of the Philippines where he took up Visual Communications. Straight out of college, he took a job as a comic book artist for a local publication. Under the pseudonym Taga-ilog, he worked for Culture Crash Comics for four years where he penned and drew his own title, "Pasig" -- a post-apocalyptic action drama. He also drew artworks for a local magazine and character designs for a Japanese animation company.

Throughout his career, he has held several comic book/animation related talks and symposiums in various schools and universities in the Philippines.

Destiny's Hand is his US debut work.

THE TREASURE CHEST

The Making of Destiny's Hand

Notes by Nunzio DeFilippis and Christina Weir
with the art of Melvin Calingo

Olivia Soldana is the 16 year old lead character of Destiny's Hand. She's the right hand woman to the Captain of the ship, and when he needs his crew to go on one last adventure in his name, she's the one he puts in charge. But the crew has difficulties following a girl, no matter how tough she might be. So in order to lead the crew to the Destiny's Hand and honor her Captain's request, Olivia's going to have to get creative.

Olivia Soldana

SEBASTIAN BLAINE'S WEAPON

→ HEAVY CURVED AXE HEAD ATTACHMENT
USED TO LOP OFF HEADS AND
EVEN SHIP MASTS!
→ BLAINE'S FAVORITE?

→ HEAVY SPEAR POINT
POKE !!

← SCREW

← SHAFT

→ 4 PRONG
SWORD MACE
ATTACHMENT
→ POKE!
TENDER!

→ SCIMITAR
ATTACHMENT
→ SLICE & DICE!

HAND SIZE

Olivia's design was the subject of a LOT of debate. Our original proposal called for something more traditionally pirate. We wanted pants (of the tight, pirate variety) and maybe an oversized shirt.

Melvin's design was far less authentic pirate, but much more what one might expect of a manga female. Jason loved it. There was a lot of back and forth, and we decided that so long as Olivia wasn't someone who conformed to how anyone expects her to dress (not her parents, and not the other pirates), it worked for us.

Melvin initially gave her two pistols, which we loved. But we also wanted her to have a blade, as the genre calls for knife and sword fighting. It was his idea to give her a blade that was essentially an attachment to Captain Blaine's own weapon. It cements the bond between the two characters and gives her a weapon that looks cool.

It was this sort of storytelling instinct that Melvin started bringing to the character design work that told us he was the right guy to tell this story with us.

Captain Sebastian Blaine is the gentleman pirate. When he comes after your vessel, you know two things. First, his ship, Destiny's Hand, cannot be sunk. The second is, if you surrender, no harm will come to you or your crew. His men will hurt no-one, claim your cargo, escort your ship safely to a port, and even tell you cool pirate stories on the way. So, as you can guess, most ships surrender to Destiny's Hand and Captain Blaine immediately. Sure, they lose cargo. But no one gets hurt and everyone gets a memorable experience.

Captain Blaine is the last of a dying breed, though. Today's pirates are meaner, more savage. They live for the fight and the thrill of the kill as much as the lure of treasure. Blaine sees the new breed as dishonorable, and wants his crew to carry on in his style of piracy. But he knows that without him to push them, they may disband and seek jobs with less honorable crews.

Melvin's design for Blaine took us by surprise. When we envisioned a gentleman pirate, we pictured someone older and more staid. But this design was SO much better than what we had in our heads. Melvin's Blaine is young, sexy, shirtless, but also very gentlemanly. It's hard to describe what it is about the design that seems so gentlemanly, but we think it jumps out at you without being definable in quick phrases. It's perfect, and our only note to Melvin was that Blaine should wear the cool coat pretty often.

Sebastian Blaine

Lady Kate is the figurehead on Destiny's Hand. Some say it's her protection that makes the ship unsinkable. Who is she? That's a question that will be explored in the story itself, so we won't give too much away. But as the designs make clear, Lady Kate is inspired by a real woman, someone who meant a lot to Captain Blaine.

Like Blaine, Melvin got Lady Kate right on the first try. The woman has a gentle charm and a beauty that we'll need - though we can't tell you why just yet.

And the figurehead has a sadness that is absolutely vital. She also looks like a beautiful figurehead, one that would look gorgeous on a real ship.

The orb in the figurehead's hands was so striking to us, we worked it into the story! When the story starts, Lady Kate's hands are empty. If the crew wants to find The Devil's Eye, that will have to change.

Lady Kate

Diego Basteon is an the ship's boatswain (pronounced bosun). Discipline is his domain on Destiny's Hand. Of Blaine's key lieutennants, he's the one who least fits the 'gentlemanly' motif. He longs for more battle, and is a bit tired of the surrenders and the entertaining of the surrendering crew. To him, this is a dog and pony show. And he'd rather face a good battle. But Diego owes his life to Blaine, and will follow his orders no matter what he thinks of them.

Diego's weapon of choice is a Cat O'Nine Tails. He uses it to maintain discipline on the ship and ensure that the crew follows Blaine's orders. Some worry he enjoys flogging disobedient sailors too much, that it's where he finds his battle since so many ships surrender to Destiny's Hand. But the crew is well-disciplined and generally he doesn't need to flog anyone, so if this is his release, Diego must be very frustrated.

Diego's character design is an example of the input Jason DeAngelis has on the creative process. The first design worked well for us, we liked what Melvin had done. But we sat down with Jason to talk character designs, and he gave notes on many of them. He wanted Diego to be more distinctive. Thus, Diego became bald. His scars became more pronounced. We suggested he lose the coat and go shirtless. The second version, does seem more distinctive, so it looks like Jason knows what he's talking about.

Lastly, Diego's last name was once Fortuna, but Jason worried that this was a pretty happy sounding name for such a grim guy. We decided Basteon would reflect his strength and dour-ness.

Diego Basteon

Frederick Matthau is Blaine's strategist and also the navigator. No one reads maps and situations as well as Matthau. In order to be a good strategist, Matthau has to be an excellent judge of character, and he is, but he's also a very solitary and lonely man. His life is the ship, and while the crew respects him, few really know him. Most of his contact is with Blaine.

Matthau is supposed to be an owl of a man, wise and stodgy. But we didn't want him to be a wimp or someone who looked out of his element on the seas. He may not be a fighter, but he always looks like he belongs on a ship. Melvin nailed all these aspects of the character on the first try, which you see here.

Melvin also succeeded in depicting a certain inner decency, which we really wanted for Matthau. In making him a little withdrawn from the crew and also a strategist, there was a chance he could have come off as manipulative. That's not in this design, and we're glad. Matthau may be the one who guides things on the ship behind the scenes, but in the end, he is 100% loyal to Blaine.

Frederik Matthau

Badru is a native from one of the local islands. He is viewed by many in the crew as a primitive, maybe even a bit savage. But he's one of the few crewmembers who can read, and despite his massive frame and skill in fighting, he doesn't tend towards violence. He admires Blaine's gentlemanly way with piracy.

Badru was completely redesigned before the sketch you see here. The first design for Badru wasn't in a design sketch. It was in a 5 page sequence done by Melvin at the very early stages of character and story breakdowns. Melvin was, we think, trying to make certain he had the job (in our minds he already had it by then, so maybe he was just flexing his sequential muscles) and he put together five pages of Olivia (then named Andrea) and Badru coming ashore to look for medicine for Blaine. It was unscripted, just stuff Melvin came up with. It was very cute stuff, and a good test drive on Olivia's look.

But Badru at the time didn't look very different, ethnically, from the rest of the crew. So when we sat down with Jason to talk designs (see our notes on Diego for more on that), one of the things we discussed was Badru. We wanted him to be an islander, with traces of Native American to his design. While Destiny's Hand is set in a fictional world with fictional ports, the feel is very Caribbean. So if you look at the setting as vaguely Caribbean, then think of Badru as a native of one of the islands like Hispaniola. Given the cues to redraw him, Melvin, as usual, hit the design out of the park. As you can see.

Badru

Ah, Owen. Owen is a bard... a scribe... a mooch. He came aboard Destiny's Hand to write a biography of the gentleman pirate. That was six years ago. He hasn't left since. He has been the 'guest' of the crew ever since. Diego has insisted that Owen pull his own weight, so he works alongside the crew on raids, and takes point in entertaining surrendered sailors.

Owen has a weakness for alcohol, and has become fascinated with the life of piracy his subject leads. He says he's still there because his story is 'ongoing.' But it's possible he's just staying because he's become one of the crew. He likes the respect he gets in the ports and especially the attention he gets from the ladies for being a pirate.

The full body design on Owen was Melvin's first try. It looked great to us. The bandolier of mini-kegs was perfect and we suddenly envisioned him drinking from them mid battle. But we also see him lighting a wick on one and tossing it at an enemy. Explosive stuff, that booze. The closeup gives you a better view of Owen's eyepatch. Some among the crew think it's fake. But no one has ever just pulled it off to check. Because if you're wrong... gross. Plus, Blaine has told the crew not to harass Owen, and that means Diego will punish anyone who does. And no one wants that.

Owen Galviston

As you can see, Melvin's designs ran with the urchin notion. He's drawn Wyatt as pretty 'Oliver Twist.' Which works for us. We also like his spiky hair which manages to be both boy-tough and androgynous at the same time. That's hard to pull off. But Melvin strikes again.

Wyatt is the lookout on Destiny's Hand. He hopes to be accepted as a topman (a crewman assigned to work on the sails) at some point, but he's not super-skilled with the sails yet. But that's where he loves to be. He loves climbing the masts and he sometimes even sleeps in the crow's nest. He's the kind of kid who always sees what he's not supposed to, not just because of his keen eyesight (which serves him well as lookout) but also because he's nosy.

Wyatt joined the crew only last year, stowing away when they were in port one day. No one knows how he got on board, and no one knows whether he was from that port or somewhere else entirely. He's never given anyone his last name. He's a runaway, a street urchin, a kid with no place to go back to, and a strong desire to be an important crewman on Destiny's Hand. Right now, he's more of a pest than anything else. But he's a useful pest.

Wyatt

Governor Thomas Houghton is the governor of St. Vickensburg, the most anti-pirate port in the area. He loathes pirates, and strives to maintain a city that is less troubled by their riff-raff and brawls. Houghton's hatred of pirates is two-fold. First, as governor, he's very law and order. But secondly, he's had personal problems with pirates in the past and has a particular hatred of Captain Blaine that goes way back. Neither man will talk about why there's bad blood between them. Both will chalk it up to Blaine being a pirate and Houghton loving law and order.

Melvin only had to do one design on Houghton. The look was perfect. In our parallel Carribean, St. Vickensburg is a 'British' port, and Houghton is supposed to be the prototypical 'English' governor. Stodgy, proper, and as concerned with making his city look good as he is with keeping it safe. Melvin managed to convey the stodgy British governor perfectly.

Another element he managed to convey is the tired-ness of Houghton. The design hints at a man who feels defeated. This was a nice touch on his part. We never called for it directly, but Melvin read the detailed bios we put together and looking at Houghton's full story, came to that on his own. He has good character instincts.

Thomas Houghton

Elias Houghton is the son of Governor Houghton and has inherited his father's distaste for pirates. But that's a problem, because Elias is the one guy who will be able to lead Destiny's Hand to the Devil's Eye. Elias is a scholar, a linguist. He's the only one Blaine knows of who is fully fluent in a now-dead tongue. Every map piece, every artifact, every clue leading to the treasure is in that tongue, so if Olivia's going to lead the crew to the treasure that Blaine wants, she's going to have to get Elias' help - whether he wants to give it or not.

Elias is a romantic interest for Olivia, and is also a dramatic and comedic foil for her. He had to be her opposite number - the complete opposite of everything she is - but in a way that generates sparks as much as it generates tension.

So Elias needed to be the anti-Olivia. She wants nothing more than to be a great pirate. He wants nothing to do with piracy. She is educated and articulate but would rather be cussing and brawling. He thinks the life of piracy is the life of illiterate degenerates. She acts first, thinks later. He thinks always. Melvin captures a sort of nebbishy cuteness with Elias that works perfectly. He looks like someone who'd look down his nose at pirates. But he's cute enough to be worthy of romantic tensions with our lead.

But Melvin also got the last, key ingredient. He also looks like someone who has a bit of pirate buried within him, doesn't he?

Elias Houghton

TREASURE CHEST

We all know, deep down inside that real pirates were probably not like Blaine. We pretend they were. In reality, too many were like this guy. Lars Mulgrew. A raping, pillaging, town-sacking, brutalizing kind of pirate who uses his crew's prowess and the freedom of the waves to do whatever he likes no matter who gets hurt or dies.

Lars Mulgrew is the new breed of pirate. He's everything that Blaine hates. Too many young pirates follow his way, the way of blood and anger. Blaine knows that Mulgrew is after the Devil's Eye, and that's at least part of the reason why he wants his crew to go after it. The Devil's Eye in Mulgrew's hand would be a disaster.

Melvin's design was not what we were expecting for Mulgrew. He drew him far sexier than we imagined. He's so sexy, in fact, that we now have to wonder about putting some sexual tension between Mulgrew and Olivia down the line. The design was so very different from what we pictured. Yet it was perfect.

In discussions with Jason, we took a good look at the full Mulgrew design and focused on the one shot of him holding up his fist. You can see there, he has an odd wrist brace. Just looking at that art spun the three of us off in random speculation. And from that was born the notion that Mulgrew has a special weapon attached to his wrist. We talked about it a lot, and what we came up with is a spring loaded grapple launcher. This can spear an enemy and then the coils will retract into the launcher, pulling that enemy towards you on the barbed end.

Melvin did a new design for the weapon. His design looks more handcuff/capture-y than spear-y. But we figure the ends of that cuff are barbed and can stick into the target. Nasty weapon, huh?

> REST MODE

> LEATHER WRIST GUARD FOR BURN PROTECTION

Lars Mulgrew

If you look back at Lars Mulgrew's design, you'll see a cool tattoo that works across his left shoulder. That's a Kraken. Mulgrew's ship is called The Kraken, named after one of the most feared mythical creatures of the deep. Since Destiny's Hand has Lady Kate, the Kraken has its own figurehead. This figurehead inspires terror in all who behold it.

Melvin did this one based on the notion that the ship was called the Kraken, but we didn't ask for a specific figurehead design. He just decided he needed to design it in advance. And he did a fine job. It looks like a real figurehead. That's an important part of what Melvin is bringing to this book. Everything piratey - the ships, the coats, the figureheads. He gives them an authenticity that says he's either really familiar with ships and the sea, or he loves pirate stories or both. He's the perfect man for the job.

The Kraken

TREASURE CHEST

The last character is Michel Langrisse. He is Captain of the defense fleet of the port of Valroux. Unlike St. Vickensberg, Valroux is a very pirate-friendly port. Pirates who respect laws while in port can come and go freely. Blaine's crew is particularly welcome because they never hurt innocents and try to avoid killing anyone.

Valroux is our "French" port. It has a more fun-loving side than the "British" port of St. Vickensburg, and anything goes there. Langrisse is well groomed and respectable, so he doesn't typify that aspect of the city. But he has a certain flexibility that allows such a port to exist and not fall into chaos. He respects the people's rights to do what they like, but knows when to put his foot down and restore order.

Langrisse cuts Destiny's Hand a lot of slack for a couple of reasons. One, as we said, they are the decent side of piracy, and he wants their ways to have rewards. The other is Olivia. Michel has a history with Olivia that will be explored. He can offer her a certain respectability to her life, if ever she wanted to settle down. Unfortunately for him, settling down is hardly on Olivia's agenda.

Our only concern with Langrisse's original design (the full design) was that he seemed a bit older than we wanted. We envisioned him just having become Captain, at maybe 20 years old or so. It was vital he not be too much older than Olivia because he needed to be a viable romantic option and not just a creepy older guy who was into teenage girls. The face designs were Melvin's second go, and all make him seem younger. We particularly like the one in the upper right and also the laughing one in the bottom left.

Michel Langrisse

The Tattoos of Destiny's Hand:

When we first came up with the characters for Destiny's Hand, we gave short descriptions and let Melvin have a go at designs. He drew basic designs for the many characters, and central to a couple of them (most importantly Olivia) were some cool tattoo designs.

We sat down with Jason DeAngelis to go over the designs, to see what we thought of them. Jason wanted everything to be as iconic as possible, and among other ideas we came up with that day (including the five fingers idea) was the idea that the key members of the crew of Destiny's Hand should have personalized tattoos.

This notion did not work its way into dialogue or plot just yet, but the tattoos are there, on the crew, an unspoken piece of detail. One day, it'll come up in plot. But for now, we'll discuss the tattoos here.

Sebastian Blaine

The choice for Blaine's tattoo was already made for us. We had asked for a skeletal hand in front of crossbones to serve as Destiny's Hand's colors. Melvin instead gave us a skeletal hand in front of crossed swords. It looked great, and the flag for the ship was one of the first designs that came in.

So when we decided each member of the crew had their own tattoo, it made perfect sense that Blaine, the ship's Captain, had the flag itself.

Even though the flag was decided upon quickly, there were still minor revisions. One of Melvin's early designs had an Ouroboros (the symbol of the snake consuming its own tail) instead of the circle behind the ship's logo. It looked really cool, but while the Ouroboros is usually a positive symbol, it still seemed to imply the crew would consume itself in some way, and we wanted Blaine's crew to not have such an ill omen.

Olivia Soldana

As we mentioned earlier, the tattoo for Olivia was part of Melvin's original design. There was some back and forth about Olivia's outfit that went into the character design discussions (we eventually went with an early Melvin design and shelved our reservations, and we have to say, she looks pretty cool). But during those discussions, one thing that never changed was the tattoo. We loved it on the first artwork he did for Olivia, and we still love it.

The crossed pistols behind the skull made such a strong impression on us, we decided that Olivia carries the pistols. So Melvin started drawing them crossed and tucked in at the back of her belt.

Diego Basteon

When we decided to create tattoos for the whole crew, we sent a 'character bible' to Melvin. It was a short list of details. It included character weapon, character tattoo, and design notes from our meeting with Jason.

On Diego, the first two categories were the same. Weapon: Cat O'Nine Tails. Tattoo: Cat O'Nine Tails

What you see is Melvin's final design. His first was as basic as our request – a simple drawing of the weapon. But this newer design has more flair to it. When the initial one came in, we heard from Jason that Melvin was tweaking it. The final version came about during the pages of Diego's fight with Olivia. We saw the art on those pages, and suddenly, Diego had a killer tattoo. The last question was size – Buckethead did two versions of the page where Diego stands ready to fight Olivia. One had the tattoo you see in the final product, the other had it way bigger. Jason suggested the final size, and Diego's tattoo was complete.

Frederick Matthau

Our tattoo note on Matthau was, as most of them were, vague, leaving some room for Melvin to get creative. We simply asked for "a map. Or maybe a compass."

What we got instead was what you see here. That was all Melvin, and his first take on the tattoo was the only one he needed, because it looks perfect.

Badru

We asked for something completely different on Badru, something that ultimately didn't work. Our initial notes called for "a skeletal arm except bones are bent to simulate a bulging muscle."

We never saw Melvin's attempts at this, but we imagine that this design proved impossible to draw as a realistic tattoo, particularly one that would show up well on the pages of a black and white manga.

Instead, Melvin went another way entirely, using our call for Native American imagery on Badru to give the big man a tattoo of another life that was nearly wiped out when white people came West – the buffalo. It symbolizes the size, strength and grace of Badru perfectly.

Owen Galviston

When we talked about Owen's design, we got very enamored of the little kegs Melvin drew on the bard's bandolier. We talked with Jason for a long time about how they could explode in battle, about comic bits of him drinking from them. We got a little obsessed with the damn things.

So when it came time for Owen's tattoo, we asked for a drawing of the mini-keg. As an afterthought, we mentioned another possible design, the Quill.

Fortunately, Melvin was not at our meeting, so he wasn't swept up in the keg hysteria and was able to see that the Quill was really the right symbol for Owen. If he'd been there with us, Owen's tattoo would probably have been a keg, which wouldn't have shown him as a writer at all, just as a lush. Nice save, Melvin.

Wyatt

In most cases, we're showing you only the final design and discussing its evolution. But this is one case where we think showing both designs will be more fun.

In our character bible, we asked for Wyatt's tattoo to be either a "crow in a nest" or an "eye." The crow in the nest proved too clunky an image, so Melvin tried the eye. This is what we got:

This is an absolutely gorgeous tattoo. We loved it. However, it is, as Jason pointed out, almost too mystical for the very simple character of Wyatt. He's a kid, and not steeped in any supernatural elements. The Egyptian motif on this eye didn't quite work with that. So Jason sent Melvin back to the drawing board, and the final result called back to the image of the crow. But it's got some flair to it, as well.

Still, we wanted Wyatt's earlier tattoo design to be shown here, because it was such a nice image for a tattoo, just ultimately not one that fit the character.

Lars Mulgrew

We know, we know, Lars Mulgrew's not a member of the crew. But still, a guy like him just demands a tattoo, you know? Mulgrew's original designs featured a tattoo on his shoulder, and even a small design by Melvin. We loved it.

So when we decided to give tattoos to the whole crew, we didn't want that to mean Mulgrew lost his. He is a pirate, after all, and it's not like Destiny's Hand invented the idea of tattoos on pirates.

Mulgrew's tattoo has since evolved a tiny bit, but this was not the result of any notes on our part. Like any talented artist, Melvin is always tweaking his stuff, looking for ways to improve it. He added the dagger to the tattoo. Looks great to us.

Elias Houghton

Elias doesn't have a tattoo when we meet him. In fact, he would shudder at the thought of getting one.

But if and when he makes any peace with the role the crew has in mind for him, they're going to insist he get one (in fact, that will probably be the point when the crew's tattoos get explained in story). So we asked for a design from Melvin to cover what tattoo the crew would force him to get.

The first design was a book with a pirate skull and crossbones on the cover. It looked good to us, but Melvin went ahead and completely redesigned. As you can see, he worked the rejected Wyatt tattoo into Elias' final design. A good artist never lets his good stuff go to waste. It works much better on Elias, given his mother's legacy.

But man is that a lot of ink! The crew may really have it in for Elias if they give him that detailed a tattoo. Perhaps Owen can give him a shot from a mini keg first.

In Volume 2 of

Destiny's HAND

Written by Nunzio DeFilippis and Christina Weir
Illustrated by Melvin Calingo

The crew of Destiny's Hand sets a course for the legendary Isle du Diablo, home of the Devil's Eye. But will their newly found scholar help them in their quest? Or will he finish off the dying Captain Blaine? And what happens when Governor Houghton comes after his son, and forces the Island of Valroux to join his anti-pirate campaign? With the governor on their heels, and a potential traitor in their midst, the crew starts a race with the Kraken for the ultimate treasure, and the winner will determine the fate of everyone on the seas!

Amazing_Agent
LUNA
volume 3

From the writers of Destiny's Hand

Volume 1 & 2 In Stores Now!

Luna: the perfect secret agent. A girl grown in a lab from the finest genetic material, she has been trained since birth to be the U.S. government's ultimate espionage weapon. But now she is given an assignment that will test her abilities to the max - high school!

story
Nunzio DeFilippis & Christina Weir • *art* Shiei

INVERLOCH   EARTHSONG

THE NET'S HOTTEST WEBCOMICS
Now In Print!

OMAKE

The following pages are Melvin Calingo's
tryout pages for Destiny's Hand and shows
the earliest incarnations of the characters.

"At this point in the production, only Olivia's
character design was finalized (her having shorts
came much later). This was also the first time I drew
Badru (even before the actual character designs.)"

- Melvin C.

4

Based on N&C's description of Badru, I conjured up a character who'd probably be snobbish but downright loyal... kinda like a pirate version of Alfred from Batman. The final version of Badru turned out to be the silent, no-nonsense, bodyguard-type... my favorite among the crew! (after Olivia of course.)

Here, she tricks the guy into arm wrestling with her because she says Badru's really sick and only has a few days to live. Badru doesn't like this one bit.

At first, I thought of Olivia as a childish pirate girl who'd use her charms more than her wits to get her way. In the book, she's far more mature and would choose finesse over charm any day.

Yup she's strong. It's probably a manga exaggeration, but it gets the point across. Read chapter 1 again and see how she kicks the cabin door into splinters!

THE END

YOU'RE READING THE WRONG WAY

This is the last page of *Destiny's Hand* Volume 1.

This book reads from right to left, Japanese style. To read from the beginning, flip the book over to the other side, start with the top right panel, and take it from there.

If this is your first time reading manga, just follow the diagram. It may seem backwards at first, but you'll get used to it! Have fun!